Think Like a Mountain

Think Like a Mountain

Essays from A Sand County Almanac

ALDO LEOPOLD

PENGUIN BOOKS — GREEN IDEAS

PENGUIN BOOKS

UK | USA | Canada | Ireland | Australia
India | New Zealand | South Africa

Penguin Books is part of the Penguin Random House group of companies
whose addresses can be found at global.penguinrandomhouse.com.

First published in *A Sand County Almanac* 2020
This extract published in Penguin Books 2021
001

Aldo Leopold's 'Land Ethic' recognizes and celebrates the interdependence between humanity and the natural world. The Aldo Leopold Foundation was established to reflect its values and continue its work: building a community that cares for people, places, and everything that connects them. Founded by Aldo and Estella Leopold's five children and designated as the executor of *A Sand County Almanac* and Leopold's other writings, the Aldo Leopold Foundation serves to preserve his legacy and vision. It also protects and manages the Leopold Shack and Farm, a National Historic Landmark. Based in Baraboo, Wisconsin, near the Shack, the Leopold Center, a green building constructed from trees the Leopold family planted, hosts thousands of visitors each year. Find out more about the foundation's program and how to get involved at www.aldoleopold.org.

Set in 11.5/14pt Dante MT Std
Typeset by Jouve (UK), Milton Keynes
Printed and bound in Great Britain by Clays Ltd, Elcograf S.p.A.

The authorized representative in the EEA is Penguin Random House Ireland,
Morrison Chambers, 32 Nassau Street, Dublin D02 YH68

A CIP catalogue record for this book is available from the British Library

ISBN: 978-0-241-51466-5

www.greenpenguin.co.uk

Penguin Random House is committed to a
sustainable future for our business, our readers
and our planet. This book is made from Forest
Stewardship Council® certified paper.

Contents

Wisconsin

Marshland Elegy

A dawn wind stirs on the great marsh. With almost imperceptible slowness it rolls a bank of fog across the wide morass. Like the white ghost of a glacier the mists advance, riding over phalanxes of tamarack, sliding across bog-meadows heavy with dew. A single silence hangs from horizon to horizon.

Out of some far recess of the sky a tinkling of little bells falls soft upon the listening land. Then again silence. Now comes a baying of some sweet-throated hound, soon the clamor of a responding pack. Then a far clear blast of hunting horns, out of the sky into the fog.

High horns, low horns, silence, and finally a pandemonium of trumpets, rattles, croaks, and cries that almost shakes the bog with its nearness, but without yet disclosing whence it comes. At last a glint of sun reveals the approach of a great echelon of birds. On motionless wing they emerge from the lifting mists, sweep a final arc of sky, and settle in clangorous descending spirals to their feeding grounds. A new day has begun on the crane marsh.

A sense of time lies thick and heavy on such a place. Yearly since the ice age it has awakened each spring to the clangor of cranes. The peat layers that comprise the bog are laid down in the basin of an ancient lake. The cranes stand, as it were, upon the sodden pages of their own history. These peats are the compressed remains of the mosses that clogged the pools, of the tamaracks that spread over the moss, of the cranes that bugled over the tamaracks since the retreat of the ice sheet. An endless caravan of generations has built of its own bones this bridge into the future, this habitat where the oncoming host again may live and breed and die.

To what end? Out on the bog a crane, gulping some luckless frog, springs his ungainly hulk into the air and flails the morning sun with mighty wings. The tamaracks re-echo with his bugled certitude. He seems to know.

Our ability to perceive quality in nature begins, as in art, with the pretty. It expands through successive stages of the beautiful to values as yet uncaptured by language. The quality of cranes lies, I think, in this higher gamut, as yet beyond the reach of words.

This much, though, can be said: our appreciation of the crane grows with the slow unraveling of earthly history. His tribe, we now know, stems out of the remote Eocene. The other members of the fauna in which he originated are long since entombed within the hills. When we hear his call we hear no mere bird. We hear the trumpet in the orchestra of evolution. He is the symbol of our untamable past, of that incredible sweep of millennia which underlies and conditions the daily affairs of birds and men.

And so they live and have their being – these cranes – not in the constricted present, but in the wider reaches of evolutionary time. Their annual return is the ticking of the geologic clock. Upon the place of their return they confer a peculiar distinction. Amid the endless mediocrity of the commonplace, a crane marsh holds a paleontological patent of nobility, won in the march of aeons, and revocable only by shotgun. The sadness discernible in some marshes arises, perhaps, from their once having harbored cranes. Now they stand humbled, adrift in history.

Some sense of this quality in cranes seems to have been felt by sportsmen and ornithologists of all ages. Upon such quarry as this the Holy Roman Emperor Frederick loosed his gyrfalcons. Upon such quarry as this once swooped the hawks of Kublai Khan. Marco Polo tells us: 'He derives the highest amusement from sporting with gyrfalcons and hawks. At Changanor the Khan has a great Palace surrounded by a fine plain where are found cranes in great numbers. He causes millet and other grains to be sown in order that the birds may not want.'

The ornithologist Bengt Berg, seeing cranes as a boy upon the Swedish heaths, forthwith made them his life work. He followed them to Africa and discovered their winter retreat on the White Nile. He says of his first encounter: 'It was a spectacle which eclipsed the flight of the roc in the *Thousand and One Nights*.'

When the glacier came down out of the north, crunching hills and gouging valleys, some adventuring rampart of the ice climbed the Baraboo Hills and fell back into the outlet gorge of the Wisconsin River. The swollen waters backed up and formed a lake half as long as the state, bordered on the east by cliffs of ice, and fed by the torrents that fell from melting mountains. The shorelines of this old lake are still visible; its bottom is the bottom of the great marsh.

The lake rose through the centuries, finally spilling over east of the Baraboo range. There it cut a new channel for the river, and thus drained itself. To the residual lagoons came the cranes, bugling the defeat of the retreating winter, summoning the on-creeping host of living things to their collective task of marsh-building. Floating bogs of sphagnum moss clogged the lowered waters, filled them. Sedge and leatherleaf, tamarack and spruce successively advanced over the bog, anchoring it by their root fabric, sucking out its water, making peat. The lagoons disappeared, but not the cranes. To the moss-meadows that replaced the ancient waterways they returned each spring to dance and bugle and rear their gangling sorrel-colored young. These, albeit birds, are not properly called chicks, but *colts*. I cannot explain why. On some dewy June morning watch them gambol over their ancestral pastures at the heels of the roan mare, and you will see for yourself.

One year not long ago a French trapper in buckskins pushed his canoe up one of the moss-clogged creeks that thread the great marsh. At this attempt to invade their miry stronghold the cranes gave vent to loud and ribald laughter. A century or two later Englishmen came in covered wagons. They chopped clearings in the timbered moraines that border the marsh, and in them planted corn and buckwheat. They did not intend, like the Great Khan at Changanor, to feed the cranes. But the cranes do not question the intent of glaciers, emperors, or pioneers. They ate the grain, and

when some irate farmer failed to concede their usu-
fruct in his corn, they trumpeted a warning and sailed
across the marsh to another farm.

There was no alfalfa in those days, and the hill-
farms made poor hay land, especially in dry years.
One dry year someone set a fire in the tamaracks. The
burn grew up quickly to bluejoint grass, which, when
cleared of dead trees, made a dependable hay meadow.
After that, each August, men appeared to cut hay. In
winter, after the cranes had gone South, they drove
wagons over the frozen bogs and hauled the hay to
their farms in the hills. Yearly they plied the marsh
with fire and axe, and in two short decades hay meadows dotted the whole expanse.

Each August when the haymakers came to pitch
their camps, singing and drinking and lashing their
teams with whip and tongue, the cranes whinnied to
their colts and retreated to the far fastnesses. 'Red
shitepokes' the haymakers called them, from the rusty
hue which at that season often stains the battleship-
gray of crane plumage. After the hay was stacked and
the marsh again their own, the cranes returned, to call
down out of October skies the migrant flocks from
Canada. Together they wheeled over the new-cut stub-
bles and raided the corn until frosts gave the signal for
the winter exodus.

These hay-meadow days were the Arcadian age for

marsh dwellers. Man and beast, plant and soil lived on and with each other in mutual toleration, to the mutual benefit of all. The marsh might have kept on producing hay and prairie chickens, deer and muskrat, crane-music and cranberries forever.

The new overlords did not understand this. They did not include soil, plants, or birds in their ideas of mutuality. The dividends of such a balanced economy were too modest. They envisaged farms not only around, but *in* the marsh. An epidemic of ditch-digging and land-booming set in. The marsh was gridironed with drainage canals, speckled with new fields and farmsteads.

But crops were poor and beset by frosts, to which the expensive ditches added an aftermath of debt. Farmers moved out. Peat beds dried, shrank, caught fire. Sun-energy out of the Pleistocene shrouded the countryside in acrid smoke. No man raised his voice against the waste, only his nose against the smell. After a dry summer not even the winter snows could extinguish the smoldering marsh. Great pockmarks were burned into field and meadow, the scars reaching down to the sands of the old lake, peat-covered these hundred centuries. Rank weeds sprang out of the ashes, to be followed after a year or two by aspen scrub. The cranes were hard put, their numbers shrinking with the remnants of unburned meadow.

For them, the song of the power shovel came near being an elegy. The high priests of progress knew nothing of cranes, and cared less. What is a species more or less among engineers? What good is an undrained marsh anyhow?

For a decade or two crops grew poorer, fires deeper, wood-fields larger, and cranes scarcer, year by year. Only reflooding, it appeared, could keep the peat from burning. Meanwhile cranberry growers had, by plugging drainage ditches, reflooded a few spots and obtained good yields. Distant politicians bugled about marginal land, over-production, unemployment relief, conservation. Economists and planners came to look at the marsh. Surveyors, technicians, CCCs, buzzed about. A counter-epidemic of reflooding set in. Government bought land, resettled farmers, plugged ditches wholesale. Slowly the bogs are rewetting. The fire-pocks become ponds. Grass fires still burn, but they can no longer burn the wetted soil.

All this, once the CCC camps were gone, was good for cranes, but not so the thickets of scrub popple that spread inexorably over the old burns, and still less the maze of new roads that inevitably follow governmental conservation. To build a road is so much simpler than to think of what the country really needs. A roadless marsh is seemingly as worthless to the alphabetical conservationist as an undrained one was to the empire-builders. Solitude, the one natural resource still undowered of alphabets, is so far recognized as valuable only by ornithologists and cranes.

Thus always does history, whether of marsh or marketplace, end in paradox. The ultimate value in these marshes is wildness, and the crane is wildness incarnate. But all conservation of wildness is self-defeating, for to cherish we must see and fondle, and when enough have seen and fondled, there is no wilderness left to cherish.

Some day, perhaps in the very process of our benefactions, perhaps in the fullness of geologic time, the last crane will trumpet his farewell and spiral skyward from the great marsh. High out of the clouds will fall the sound of hunting horns, the baying of the phantom pack, the tinkle of little bells, and then a silence never to be broken, unless perchance in some far pasture of the Milky Way.

The Sand Counties

Every profession keeps a small herd of epithets, and needs a pasture where they may run at large. Thus economists must find free range somewhere for their pet aspersions, such as sub-marginality, regression, and institutional rigidity. Within the ample reaches of the Sand Counties these economic terms of reproach find beneficial exercise, free pasturage, and immunity from the gadflies of critical rebuttal.

Soil experts, likewise, would have a hard life without the Sand Counties. Where else would their podzols, gleys, and anaerobics find a living?

Social planners have, of late years, come to use the Sand Counties for a different, albeit somewhat parallel, purpose. The sandy region serves as a pale blank area, of pleasing shape and size, on those polka-dot maps where each dot represents ten bathtubs, or five women's auxiliaries, or one mile of blacktop, or a share in a blooded bull. Such maps would become monotonous if stippled uniformly.

In short, the Sand Counties are poor.

Yet in the 1930s, when the alphabetical uplifts galloped like forty horsemen across the Big Flats, exhorting the sand farmers to resettle elsewhere, these benighted folk did not want to go, even when baited with 3 per cent at the federal land bank. I began to wonder why, and finally, to settle the question, I bought myself a sand farm.

Sometimes in June, when I see unearned dividends of dew hung on every lupine, I have doubts about the real poverty of the sands. On solvent farmlands lupines do not even grow, much less collect a daily

rainbow of jewels. If they did, the weed-control officer, who seldom sees a dewy dawn, would doubtless
insist that they be cut. Do economists known about
lupines?

Perhaps the farmers who did not want to move out
of the Sand Counties had some deep reason, rooted far
back in history, for preferring to stay. I am reminded
of this every April when the pasque-flowers bloom on
every gravelly ridge. Pasques do not say much, but I
infer that their preference harks back to the glacier
that put the gravel there. Only gravel ridges are poor
enough to offer pasques full elbow-room in April sun.
They endure snows, sleets, and bitter winds for the
privilege of blooming alone.

There are other plants who seem to ask of this
world not riches but room. Such is the little sandwort
that throws a white-lace cap over the poorest hilltops
just before the lupines splash them with blue. Sand-
worts simply refuse to live on a good farm, even on a
very good farm, complete with rock garden and
begonias. And then there is the little Linaria, so small,
so slender, and so blue that you don't even see it until
it is directly underfoot; who ever saw a Linaria except
on a sandblow?

Finally there is Draba, beside whom even Linaria is
tall and ample. I have never met an economist who
knows Draba, but if I were one I should do all my

economic pondering lying prone on the sand, with Draba at nose-length.

There are birds that are found only in the Sand Counties, for reasons sometimes easy, sometimes difficult, to guess. The clay-colored sparrow is there, for the clear reason that he is enamored of jackpines, and jackpines of sand. The sandhill crane is there, for the clear reason that he is enamored of solitude, and there is none left elsewhere. But why do woodcocks prefer to nest in the sandy regions? Their preference is rooted in no such mundane matter as food, for earthworms are far more abundant on better soils. After years of study, I now think I know the reason. The male woodcock, while doing his peenting prologue to the sky dance, is like a short lady in high heels: he does not show up to advantage in dense tangled ground cover. But on the poorest sand-streak of the poorest pasture or meadow of the Sand Counties, there is, in April at least, no ground cover at all, save only moss, Draba, cardamine, sheep-sorrel, and Antennaria, all negligible impediments to a bird with short legs. Here the male woodcock can puff and strut and mince, not only without let or hindrance, but in full view of his audience, real or hoped-for. This little circumstance, important for only an hour a day, for only one month of the year, perhaps for only one of the two sexes, and certainly wholly irrelevant to economic standards of living, determines the woodcock's choice of a home.

The economists have not yet tried to resettle woodcocks.

Odyssey

X had marked time in the limestone ledge since the Paleozoic seas covered the land. Time, to an atom locked in a rock, does not pass.

The break came when a bur-oak root nosed down a crack and began prying and sucking. In the flash of a century the rock decayed, and X was pulled out and up into the world of living things. He helped build a flower, which became an acorn, which fattened a deer, which fed an Indian, all in a single year.

From his berth in the Indian's bones, X joined again in chase and flight, feast and famine, hope and fear. He felt these things as changes in the little chemical pushes and pulls that tug timelessly at every atom. When the Indian took his leave of the prairie, X moldered briefly underground, only to embark on a second trip through the bloodstream of the land.

This time it was a rootlet of bluestem that sucked him up and lodged him in a leaf that rode the green billows of the prairie June, sharing the common task of hoarding sunlight. To this leaf also fell an uncommon task: flicking shadows across a plover's eggs. The ecstatic plover, hovering overhead, poured praises on something perfect: perhaps the eggs, perhaps the shadows, or perhaps the haze of pink phlox that lay on the prairie.

When the departing plovers set wing for the Argentine, all the bluestems waved farewell with tall new tassels. When the first geese came out of the north and all the bluestems glowed wine-red, a forehanded deermouse cut the leaf in which X lay, and buried it in an underground nest, as if to hide a bit of Indian summer from the thieving frosts. But a fox detained the mouse, molds and fungi took the nest apart, and X lay in the soil again, foot-loose and fancy-free.

Next he entered a tuft of side-oats grama, a buffalo, a buffalo chip, and again the soil. Next a spiderwort, a rabbit, and an owl. Thence a tuft of sporobolus.

All routines come to an end. This one ended with a prairie fire, which reduced the prairie plants to smoke, gas, and ashes. Phosphorus and potash atoms stayed in the ash, but the nitrogen atoms were gone with the wind. A spectator might, at this point, have predicted an early end of the biotic drama, for with fires exhausting the nitrogen, the soil might well have lost its plants and blown away.

But the prairie had two strings to its bow. Fires

thinned its grasses, but they thickened its stand of leg-
uminous herbs: prairie clover, bush clover, wild bean,
vetch, lead-plant, trefoil, and Baptisia, each carrying its
own bacteria housed in nodules on its rootlets. Each
nodule pumped nitrogen out of the air into the plant,
and then ultimately into the soil. Thus the prairie sav-
ings bank took in more nitrogen from its legumes than
it paid out to its fires. That the prairie is rich is known
to the humblest deermouse; why the prairie is rich is a
question seldom asked in all the still lapse of ages.

Between each of his excursions through the biota,
X lay in the soil and was carried by the rains, inch by
inch, downhill. Living plants retarded the wash by
impounding atoms; dead plants by locking them to
their decayed tissues. Animals ate the plants and carried them briefly uphill or downhill, depending on
whether they died or defecated higher or lower than
they fed. No animal was aware that the altitude of his
death was more important than his manner of dying.
Thus a fox caught a gopher in a meadow, carrying X
uphill to his bed on the brow of a ledge, where an
eagle laid him low. The dying fox sensed the end of his
chapter in foxdom, but not the new beginning in the
odyssey of an atom.

An Indian eventually inherited the eagle's plumes,
and with them propitiated the Fates, whom he assumed
had a special interest in Indians. It did not occur to him

that they might be busy casting dice against gravity; that mice and men, soils and songs, might be merely ways to retard the march of atoms to the sea.

One year, while X lay in a cottonwood by the river, he was eaten by a beaver, an animal that always feeds higher than he dies. The beaver starved when his pond dried up during a bitter frost. X rode the carcass down the spring freshet, losing more altitude each hour than heretofore in a century. He ended up in the silt of a backwater bayou, where he fed a crayfish, a coon, and then an Indian, who laid him down to his last sleep in a mound on the riverbank. One spring an oxbow caved the bank, and after one short week of freshet X lay again in his ancient prison, the sea.

An atom at large in the biota is too free to know freedom; an atom back in the sea has forgotten it. For every atom lost to the sea, the prairie pulls another out of the decaying rocks. The only certain truth is that its creatures must suck hard, live fast, and die often, lest its losses exceed its gains.

It is the nature of roots to nose into cracks. When Y was thus released from the parent ledge, a new animal had arrived and begun redding up the prairie to fit his own notions of law and order. An oxteam turned the prairie sod, and Y began a succession of dizzy annual trips through a new grass called wheat.

The old prairie lived by the diversity of its plants and animals, all of which were useful because the sum total of their co-operations and competitions achieved continuity. But the wheat farmer was a builder of categories; to him only wheat and oxen were useful. He saw the useless pigeons settle in clouds upon his wheat, and shortly cleared the skies of them. He saw the chinch bugs take over the stealing job, and fumed because here was a useless thing too small to kill. He failed to see the downward wash of over-wheated loam, laid bare in spring against the pelting rains. When soil-wash and chinch bugs finally put an end to wheat farming, Y and his like had already traveled far down the watershed.

When the empire of wheat collapsed, the settler took a leaf from the old prairie book: he impounded his fertility in livestock, he augmented it with nitrogen-pumping alfalfa, and he tapped the lower layers of the loam with deep-rooted corn.

But he used his alfalfa, and every other new weapon against wash, not only to hold his old plowings, but also to exploit new ones which, in turn, needed holding.

So, despite alfalfa, the black loam grew gradually thinner. Erosion engineers built dams and terraces to hold it. Army engineers built levees and wing-dams to flush it from the rivers. The rivers would not flush, but raised their beds instead, thus choking navigation.

So the engineers built pools like gigantic beaver ponds, and Y landed in one of these, his trip from rock to river completed in one short century.

On first reaching the pool, Y made several trips through water plants, fish, and waterfowl. But engineers build sewers as well as dams, and down them comes the loot of all the far hills and the sea. The atoms that once grew pasque-flowers to greet the returning plovers now lie inert, confused, imprisoned in oily sludge.

Roots still nose among the rocks. Rains still pelt the fields. Deermice still hide their souvenirs of Indian summer. Old men who helped destroy the pigeons still recount the glory of the fluttering hosts. Black and white buffalo pass in and out of red barns, offering free rides to itinerant atoms.

On a Monument to the Pigeon*

We have erected a monument to commemorate the funeral of a species. It symbolizes our sorrow. We grieve because no living man will see again the onrushing

---

* The monument to the Passenger Pigeon, placed in Wyalusing State Park, Wisconsin, by the Wisconsin Society for Ornithology. Dedicated 11 May 1947.

phalanx of victorious birds, sweeping a path for spring across the March skies, chasing the defeated winter from all the woods and prairies of Wisconsin.

Men still live who, in their youth, remember pigeons. Trees still live who, in their youth, were shaken by a living wind. But a decade hence only the oldest oaks will remember, and at long last only the hills will know.

There will always be pigeons in books and in museums, but these are effigies and images, dead to all hardships and to all delights. Book-pigeons cannot dive out of a cloud to make the deer run for cover, or clap their wings in thunderous applause of mast-laden woods. Book-pigeons cannot breakfast on new-mown wheat in Minnesota, and dine on blueberries in Canada. They know no urge of seasons; they feel no kiss of sun, no lash of wind and weather. They live forever by not living at all.

Our grandfathers were less well-housed, well-fed, well-clothed than we are. The strivings by which they bettered their lot are also those which deprived us of pigeons. Perhaps we now grieve because we are not sure, in our hearts, that we have gained by the exchange. The gadgets of industry bring us more comforts than the pigeons did, but do they add as much to the glory of the spring?

It is a century now since Darwin gave us the first

glimpse of the origin of species. We know now what was unknown to all the preceding caravan of generations: that men are only fellow-voyagers with other creatures in the odyssey of evolution. This new knowledge should have given us, by this time, a sense of kinship with fellow-creatures; a wish to live and let live; a sense of wonder over the magnitude and duration of the biotic enterprise.

Above all we should, in the century since Darwin, have come to know that man, while now captain of the adventuring ship, is hardly the sole object of its quest, and that his prior assumptions to this effect arose from the simple necessity of whistling in the dark.

These things, I say, should have come to us. I fear they have not come to many.

For one species to mourn the death of another is a new thing under the sun. The Cro-Magnon who slew the last mammoth thought only of steaks. The sportsman who shot the last pigeon thought only of his prowess. The sailor who clubbed the last auk thought of nothing at all. But we, who have lost our pigeons, mourn the loss. Had the funeral been ours, the pigeons would hardly have mourned us. In this fact, rather than in Mr DuPont's nylons or Mr Vannevar Bush's bombs, lies objective evidence of our superiority over the beasts.

★

This monument, perched like a duckhawk on this cliff, will scan this wide valley, watching through the days and years. For many a March it will watch the geese go by, telling the river about clearer, colder, lonelier waters on the tundra. For many an April it will see the redbuds come and go, and for many a May the flush of oak-blooms on a thousand hills. Questing wood ducks will search these basswoods for hollow limbs; golden prothonotaries will shake golden pollen from the river willows. Egrets will pose on these sloughs in August; plovers will whistle from September skies. Hickory nuts will plop into October leaves, and hail will rattle in November woods. But no pigeons will pass, for there are no pigeons, save only this flightless one, graven in bronze on this rock. Tourists will read this inscription, but their thoughts will not take wing.

We are told by economic moralists that to mourn the pigeon is mere nostalgia; that if the pigeoners had not done away with him, the farmers would ultimately have been obliged, in self-defense, to do so.

This is one of those peculiar truths that are valid, but not for the reasons alleged.

The pigeon was a biological storm. He was the lightning that played between two opposing potentials of intolerable intensity: the fat of the land and the oxygen of the air. Yearly the feathered tempest roared up, down, and across the continent, sucking up the laden fruits of forest and prairie, burning them in a traveling blast of life. Like any other chain reaction, the pigeon could survive no dimunition of his own furious intensity. When the pigeoners subtracted from his numbers, and the pioneers chopped gaps in the continuity of his fuel, his flame guttered out with hardly a sputter or even a wisp of smoke.

Today the oaks still flaunt their burden at the sky, but the feathered lightning is no more. Worm and weevil must now perform slowly and silently the biological task that once drew thunder from the firmament.

The wonder is not that the pigeon went out, but that he ever survived through all the millennia of pre-Babbittian time.

The pigeon loved his land: he lived by the intensity of his desire for clustered grape and bursting beechnut, and by his contempt of miles and seasons. Whatever Wisconsin did not offer him gratis today, he sought and found tomorrow in Michigan, or Labrador, or Tennessee. His love was for present things, and these things were present somewhere; to find them required only the free sky, and the will to ply his wings.

To love what *was* is a new thing under the sun, unknown to most people and to all pigeons. To see

America as history, to conceive of destiny as a becoming, to smell a hickory tree through the still lapse of ages – all these things are possible for us, and to achieve them takes only the free sky, and the will to ply our wings. In these things, and not in Mr Bush's bombs and Mr DuPont's nylons, lies objective evidence of our superiority over the beasts.

Flambeau

People who have never canoed a wild river, or who have done so only with a guide in the stern, are apt to assume that novelty, plus healthful exercise, account for the value of the trip. I thought so too, until I met the two college boys on the Flambeau.

Supper dishes washed, we sat on the bank watching a buck dunking for water plants on the far shore. Soon the buck raised his head, cocked his ears upstream, and then bounded for cover.

Around the bend now came the cause of his alarm: two boys in a canoe. Spying us, they edged in to pass the time of day.

'What time is it?' was their first question. They explained that their watches had run down, and for the first time in their lives there was no clock, whistle, or radio to set watches by. For two days they had lived by 'sun-time', and were getting a thrill out of it. No servant brought them meals: they got their meat out of the river, or went without. No traffic cop whistled them off the hidden rock in the next rapids. No friendly roof kept them dry when they misguessed whether or not to pitch the tent. No guide showed them which camping spots offered a nightlong breeze, and which a nightlong misery of mosquitoes; which firewood made clean coals, and which only smoke.

Before our young adventurers pushed off downstream, we learned that both were slated for the Army upon the conclusion of their trip. Now the *motif* was clear. This trip was their first and last taste of freedom, an interlude between two regimentations: the campus and the barracks. The elemental simplicities of wilderness travel were thrills not only because of their novelty, but because they represented complete freedom to make mistakes. The wilderness gave them their first taste of those rewards and penalties for wise and foolish acts which every woodsman faces daily, but against which civilization has built a thousand buffers. These boys were 'on their own' in this particular sense.

Perhaps every youth needs an occasional wilderness trip, in order to learn the meaning of this particular freedom.

When I was a small boy, my father used to describe

all choice camps, fishing waters, and woods as 'nearly as good as the Flambeau'. When I finally launched my own canoe in this legendary stream, I found it up to expectations as a river, but as a wilderness it was on its last legs. New cottages, resorts, and highway bridges were chopping up the wild stretches into shorter and shorter segments. To run down the Flambeau was to be mentally whipsawed between alternating impressions: no sooner had you built up the mental illusion of being in the wilds than you sighted a boat-landing, and soon you were coasting past some cottager's peonies.

Safely past the peonies, a buck bounding up the bank helped us to restore the wilderness flavor, and the next rapids finished the job. But staring at you beside the pool below was a synthetic log cabin, complete with composition roof, 'Bide-A-Wee' signboard, and rustic pergola for afternoon bridge.

Paul Bunyan was too busy a man to think about posterity, but if he had asked to reserve a spot for posterity to see what the old north woods looked like, he likely would have chosen the Flambeau, for here the cream of the white pine grew on the same acres with the cream of the sugar maple, yellow birch, and hemlock. This rich intermixture of pine and hardwoods was and is uncommon. The Flambeau pines, growing on a hardwood soil richer than pines are ordinarily able to occupy, were so large and valuable, and so close to a good log-driving stream, that they were cut at an early day, as evidenced by the decayed condition of their giant stumps. Only defective pines were spared, but there are enough of these alive today to punctuate the skyline of the Flambeau with many a green monument to bygone days.

The hardwood logging came much later; in fact, the last big hardwood company 'pulled steel' on its last logging railroad only a decade ago. All that remains of that company today is a 'land-office' in its ghost town, selling off its cutovers to hopeful settlers. Thus died an epoch in American history: the epoch of cut out and get out.

Like a coyote rummaging in the offal of a deserted camp, the post-logging economy of the Flambeau subsists on the leavings of its own past. 'Gypo' pulpwood cutters nose around in the slashings for the occasional small hemlock overlooked in the main logging. A portable sawmill crew dredges the riverbed for sunken 'deadheads', many of which drowned during the hell-for-leather log-drives of the glory days. Rows of these mud-stained corpses are drawn up on shore at the old landings – all in perfect condition, and some of great value, for no such pine exists in the north woods today. Post and pole cutters strip the swamps of white cedar; the deer follow them around and strip the felled tops of their foliage. Everybody and everything sub-sists on leavings.

So complete are all these scavengings that when the modern cottager builds a log cabin, he uses imitation logs sawed out of slab piles in Idaho or Oregon, and hauled to Wisconsin woods in a freight car. The pro-verbial coals to Newcastle seem a mild irony compared with this.

Yet there remains the river, in a few spots hardly changed since Paul Bunyan's day; at early dawn, before the motor boats awaken, one can still hear it singing in the wilderness. There are a few sections of uncut timber, luckily state-owned. And there is a con-siderable remnant of wildlife: muskellunge, bass, and sturgeon in the river; mergansers, black ducks, and wood ducks breeding in the sloughs; ospreys, eagles, and ravens cruising overhead. Everywhere are deer, perhaps too many: I counted 52 in two days afloat. A wolf or two still roams the upper Flambeau, and there is a trapper who claims he saw a marten, though no marten skin has come out of the Flambeau since 1900.

Using these remnants of the wilderness as a nucleus, the State Conservation Department began, in 1943, to rebuild a fifty-mile stretch of river as a wild area for the use and enjoyment of young Wisconsin. This wild stretch is set in a matrix of state forest, but there is to be no forestry on the riverbanks, and as few road crossings as possible. Slowly, patiently, and sometimes expensively the Conservation Department has been buying land, removing cottages, warding off unnecessary roads, and in general pushing the clock back, as far as possible, toward the original wilderness.

The good soil that enabled the Flambeau to grow the best cork pine for Paul Bunyan likewise enabled Rusk County, during recent decades, to sprout a dairy industry. These dairy farmers wanted cheaper electric power than that offered by local power companies, hence they organized a co-operative REA and in 1947 applied for a power dam, which, when built, would clip off the lower reaches of a fifty-mile stretch in process of restoration as canoe-water.

There was a sharp and bitter political fight. The Legislature, sensitive to farmer-pressure but oblivious of wilderness values, not only approved the REA dam, but deprived the Conservation Commission of any future voice in the disposition of power sites. It thus seems likely that the remaining canoe-water on the Flambeau, as well as every other stretch of wild river in the state, will ultimately be harnessed for power.

Perhaps our grandsons, having never seen a wild river, will never miss the chance to set a canoe in singing waters.

Illinois and Iowa

Illinois Bus Ride

A farmer and his son are out in the yard, pulling a crosscut saw through the innards of an ancient cottonwood. The tree is so large and so old that only a foot of blade is left to pull on.

Time was when that tree was a buoy in the prairie sea. George Rogers Clark may have camped under it; buffalo may have nooned in its shade, switching flies. Every spring it roosted fluttering pigeons. It is the best historical library short of the State College, but once a year it sheds cotton on the farmer's window screens. Of these two facts, only the second is important.

The State College tells farmers that Chinese elms do not clog screens, and hence are preferable to cottonwoods. It likewise pontificates on cherry preserves, Bang's disease, hybrid corn, and beautifying the farm home. The only thing it does not know about farms is where they came from. Its job is to make Illinois safe for soybeans.

I am sitting in a 60-mile-an-hour bus sailing over a highway originally laid out for horse and buggy. The ribbon of concrete has been widened and widened until the field fences threaten to topple into the road cuts. In the narrow thread of sod between the shaved banks and the toppling fences grow the relics of what once was Illinois: the prairie.

No one in the bus sees these relics. A worried farmer, his fertilizer bill projecting from his shirt pocket, looks blankly at the lupines, lespedezas, or Baptisias that originally pumped nitrogen out of the prairie air and into his black loamy acres. He does not distinguish them from the parvenu quack-grass in which they grow. Were I to ask him why his corn makes a hundred bushels, while that of non-prairie states does well to make thirty, he would probably answer that Illinois soil is better. Were I to ask him the name of that white spike of pea-like flowers hugging the fence, he would shake his head. A weed, likely.

A cemetery flashes by, its borders alight with prairie puccoons. There are no puccoons elsewhere; dog-fennels and sowthistles supply the yellow *motif* for the modern landscape. Puccoons converse only with the dead.

Through the open window I hear the heart-stirring whistle of an upland plover; time was when his forebears followed the buffalo as they trudged shoulder-deep through an illimitable garden of forgotten blooms. A boy spies the bird and remarks to his father: there goes a snipe.

The sign says, 'You are entering the Green River Soil Conservation District'. In smaller type is a list of who is co-operating; the letters are too small to be read from a moving bus. It must be a roster of who's who in conservation.

The sign is neatly painted. It stands in a creek-bottom pasture so short you could play golf on it. Nearby is the graceful loop of an old dry creek bed. The new creek bed is ditched straight as a ruler; it has been 'uncurled' by the county engineer to hurry the run-off. On the hill in the background are contoured strip-crops; they have been 'curled' by the erosion engineer to retard the run-off. The water must be confused by so much advice.

Everything on this farm spells money in the bank. The farmstead abounds in fresh paint, steel, and concrete. A date on the barn commemorates the founding fathers. The roof bristles with lightning rods, the weathercock is proud with new gilt. Even the pigs look solvent.

The old oaks in the woodlot are without issue. There are no hedges, brush patches, fencerows, or other signs of shiftless husbandry. The cornfield has fat steers, but probably no quail. The fences stand on narrow ribbons of sod; whoever plowed that close to barbed wires must have been saying, 'Waste not, want not'.

In the creek-bottom pasture, flood trash is lodged high in the bushes. The creek banks are raw; chunks of Illinois have sloughed off and moved seaward. Patches of giant ragweed mark where freshets have thrown down the silt they could not carry. Just who is solvent? For how long?

The highway stretches like a taut tape across the corn, oats, and clover fields; the bus ticks off the opulent miles; the passengers talk and talk and talk. About what? About baseball, taxes, sons-in-law, movies, motors, and funerals, but never about the heaving groundswell of Illinois that washes the windows of the speeding bus. Illinois has no genesis, no history, no shoals or deeps, no tides of life and death. To them Illinois is only the sea on which they sail to ports unknown.

Red Legs Kicking

When I call to mind my earliest impressions, I wonder whether the process ordinarily referred to as growing up is not actually a process of growing down; whether experience, so much touted among adults as the thing children lack, is not actually a progressive dilution of the essentials by the trivialities of living. This much at least is sure: my earliest impressions of wildlife and its pursuit retain a vivid sharpness of form, color, and atmosphere that half a century of professional wildlife experience has failed to obliterate or to improve upon.

Like most aspiring hunters, I was given, at an early age, a single-barreled shotgun and permission to hunt rabbits. One winter Saturday, *en route* to my favorite rabbit patch, I noticed that the lake, then covered with ice and snow, had developed a small 'airhole' at a point where a windmill discharged warm water from the shore. All ducks had long since departed southward, but I then and there formulated my first ornithological hypothesis: if there were a duck left in the region, he (or she) would inevitably, sooner or later, drop in at this airhole. I suppressed my appetite for rabbits (then no mean feat), sat down in the cold smartweeds on the frozen mud, and waited.

I waited all afternoon, growing colder with each passing crow, and with each rheumatic groan of the laboring windmill. Finally, at sunset, a lone black duck came out of the west, and without even a preliminary circling of the airhole, set his wings and pitched downward.

I cannot remember the shot; I remember only my

unspeakable delight when my first duck hit the snowy ice with a thud and lay there, belly up, red legs kicking.

When my father gave me the shotgun, he said I might hunt partridges with it, but that I might not shoot them from trees. I was old enough, he said, to learn wing-shooting.

My dog was good at treeing partridge, and to forego a sure shot in the tree in favor of a hopeless one at the fleeing bird was my first exercise in ethical codes. Compared with a treed partridge, the devil and his seven kingdoms was a mild temptation.

At the end of my second season of featherless partridge-hunting I was walking, one day, through an aspen thicket when a big partridge rose with a roar at my left, and, towering over the aspens, crossed behind me, hell-bent for the nearest cedar swamp. It was a swinging shot of the sort the partridge-hunter dreams about, and the bird tumbled dead in a shower of feathers and golden leaves.

I could draw a map today of each clump of red bunchberry and each blue aster that adorned the mossy spot where he lay, my first partridge on the wing. I suspect my present affection for bunchberries and asters dates from that moment.

Arizona and New Mexico

On Top

When I first lived in Arizona, the White Mountain was a horseman's world. Except along a few main routes, it was too rough for wagons. There were no cars. It was too big for foot travel; even sheepherders rode. Thus by elimination, the county-sized plateau known as 'on top' was the exclusive domain of the mounted man: mounted cowman, mounted sheepman, mounted forest officer, mounted trapper, and those unclassified mounted men of unknown origin and uncertain destination always found on frontiers. It is difficult for this generation to understand this aristocracy of space based upon transport.

No such thing existed in the railroad towns two days to the north, where you had your choice of travel by shoe leather, burro, cowhorse, buckboard, freight wagon, caboose, or Pullman. Each of these modes of movement corresponded to a social caste, the members of which spoke a distinctive vernacular, wore distinctive clothes, ate distinctive food, and patronized different saloons. Their only common denominator was a democracy of debt to the general store, and a communal wealth of Arizona dust and Arizona sunshine.

As one proceeded southward across the plains and mesas toward the White Mountain, these castes dropped out one by one as their respective modes of travel became impossible, until finally, 'on top', the horseman ruled the world.

Henry Ford's revolution has of course abolished all this. Today the plane has given even the sky to Tom, Dick, and Harry.

In winter the top of the mountain was denied even to horsemen, for the snow piled deep on the high meadows, and the little canyons up which the only trails ascended drifted full to the brim. In May every canyon roared with an icy torrent, but soon thereafter you could 'top out' – if your horse had the heart to climb half a day through knee-deep mud.

In the little village at the foot of the mountain there existed, each spring, a tacit competition to be the first rider to invade the high solitudes. Many of us tried it, for reasons we did not stop to analyze. Rumor ran fast. Whoever did it first wore a kind of horseman's halo. He was 'man-of-the-year'.

The mountain spring, storybooks to the contrary notwithstanding, did not come with a rush. Balmy days alternated with bitter winds, even after the sheep had gone up. I have seen few colder sights than a drab gray mountain meadow, sprinkled with complaining ewes and half-frozen lambs, pelted by hail and snow. Even the gay nutcrackers humped their backs to these spring storms.

The mountain in summer had as many moods as there were days and weathers; the dullest rider, as well as his horse, felt these moods to the marrow of his bones.

On a fair morning the mountain invited you to get down and roll in its new grass and flowers (your less inhibited horse did just this if you failed to keep a tight rein). Every living thing sang, chirped, and burgeoned. Massive pines and firs, storm-tossed these many months, soaked up the sun in towering dignity. Tassel-eared squirrels, poker-faced but exuding emotion with voice and tail, told you insistently what you already knew full well: that never had there been so rare a day, or so rich a solitude to spend it in.

An hour later, thunderheads may have blotted out the sun, while your erstwhile paradise cowered under the impending lash of lightning, rain, and hail. Black gloom hung poised, as over a bomb with the fuse lighted. Your horse jumped at every rolling pebble, every crackling twig. When you turned in the saddle to unlash your slicker, he shied, snorted, and trembled as if you were about to unfurl the scroll of an Apocalypse. When I hear anyone say he does not fear lightning, I still remark inwardly: he has never ridden The Mountain in July.

The explosions are fearsome enough, but more so are the smoking slivers of stone that sing past your ear when the bolt crashes into a rimrock. Still more so are the splinters that fly when a bolt explodes a pine. I remember one gleaming white one, 15 feet long, that stabbed deep into the earth at my feet and stood there humming like a tuning fork.

It must be poor life that achieves freedom from fear.

The top of the mountain was a great meadow, half a day's ride across, but do not picture it as a single amphitheater of grass, hedged in by a wall of pines. The edges of that meadow were scrolled, curled, and crenulated with an infinity of bays and coves, points and stringers, peninsulas and parks, each one of which differed from all the rest. No man knew them all, and every day's ride offered a gambler's chance of finding a new one. I say 'new' because one often had the feeling, riding into some flower-spangled cove, that if anyone had ever been here before, he must of necessity have sung a song, or written a poem.

This feeling of having this day discovered the incredible accounts, perhaps, for the profusion of initials, dates, and cattle brands inscribed on the patient bark of aspens at every mountain camp site. In these inscriptions one could, in any day, read the history of *Homo texanus* and his culture, not in the cold categories of anthropology, but in terms of the individual career of some founding father whose initials you recognized as the man whose son bested you at horse-trading, or whose daughter you once danced with. Here, dated in the nineties, was his simple initial, without brand, inscribed no doubt when he first arrived alone on the mountain as an itinerant cowpuncher. Next, a decade later, his initial plus brand; by that time he had become a solid citizen with an 'outfit', acquired by thrift, natural increase, and perhaps a nimble rope. Next, only a few years old, you found his daughter's initial, inscribed by some enamored youth aspiring not only to the lady's hand, but to the economic succession.

The old man was dead now; in his later years his heart had thrilled only to his bank account and to the tally of his flocks and herds, but the aspen revealed that in his youth he too had felt the glory of the mountain spring.

The history of the mountain was written not only in aspen bark, but in its place names. Cow-country place names are lewd, humorous, ironic, or sentimental, but seldom trite. Usually they are subtle enough to draw inquiry from new arrivals, whereby hangs that web of tales which, full spun, constitutes the local folk-lore.

For example, there was 'The Boneyard', a lovely meadow where bluebells arched over the half-buried skulls and scattered vertebrae of cows long since dead. Here in the 1880s a foolish cowman, newly arrived from the warm valleys of Texas, had trusted the allurements of the mountain summer and essayed to winter his herd on mountain hay. When the November storms hit, he and his horse had floundered out, but not his cows.

Again, there was 'The Campbell Blue', a headwater of the Blue River to which an early cowman had brought himself a bride. The lady, tiring of rocks and trees, had yearned for a piano. A piano was duly fetched, a Campbell piano. There was only one mule in the county capable of packing it, and only one packer capable of the almost superhuman task of balancing such a load. But the piano failed to bring contentment; the lady decamped; and when the story was told me, the ranch cabin was already a ruin of sagging logs.

Again there was 'Frijole Cienega', a marshy meadow walled in by pines, under which stood, in my day, a small log cabin used by any passer-by as an overnight camp. It was the unwritten law for the owner of such real estate to leave flour, lard, and beans, and for the passer-by to replenish such stock as he could. But one luckless traveler, trapped there for a week by storms, had found only beans. This breach of hospitality was sufficiently notable to be handed down to history as a place name.

Finally, there was 'Paradise Ranch', an obvious platitude when read from a map, but something quite different when you arrived there at the end of a hard ride. It lay tucked away on the far side of a high peak, as any proper paradise should. Through its verdant meadows meandered a singing trout stream. A horse left for a month on this meadow waxed so fat that rain-water gathered in a pool on his back. After my first visit to Paradise Ranch I remarked to myself: what else *could* you call it?

Despite several opportunities to do so, I have never returned to the White Mountain. I prefer not to see what tourists, roads, sawmills, and logging railroads have done for it, or to it. I hear young people, not yet born when I first rode out 'on top', exclaim about it as a wonderful place. To this, with an unspoken mental reservation, I agree.

Thinking Like a Mountain

A deep chesty bawl echoes from rimrock to rimrock, rolls down the mountain, and fades into the far blackness of the night. It is an outburst of wild defiant sorrow, and of contempt for all the adversities of the world.

Every living thing (and perhaps many a dead one as well) pays heed to that call. To the deer it is a reminder of the way of all flesh, to the pine a forecast of midnight scuffles and of blood upon the snow, to the coyote a promise of gleanings to come, to the cowman a threat of red ink at the bank, to the hunter a challenge of fang against bullet. Yet behind these obvious and immediate hopes and fears there lies a deeper meaning, known only to the mountain itself. Only the mountain has lived long enough to listen objectively to the howl of a wolf.

Those unable to decipher the hidden meaning know nevertheless that it is there, for it is felt in all wolf country, and distinguishes that country from all other land. It tingles in the spine of all who hear wolves by night, or who scan their tracks by day. Even without sight or sound of wolf, it is implicit in a hundred small events: the midnight whinny of a pack horse, the rattle of rolling rocks, the bound of a fleeing deer, the way shadows lie under the spruces. Only the ineducable tyro can fail to sense the presence or absence of wolves, or the fact that mountains have a secret opinion about them.

My own conviction on this score dates from the day I saw a wolf die. We were eating lunch on a high rimrock, at the foot of which a turbulent river elbowed its way. We saw what we thought was a doe fording the torrent, her breast awash in white water. When she climbed the bank toward us and shook out her tail, we realized our error: it was a wolf. A half-dozen others, evidently grown pups, sprang from the willows and all joined in a welcoming mêlée of wagging tails and playful maulings. What was literally a pile of wolves writhed and tumbled in the center of an open flat at the foot of our rimrock.

In those days we had never heard of passing up a chance to kill a wolf. In a second we were pumping lead into the pack, but with more excitement than accuracy: how to aim a steep downhill shot is always confusing. When our rifles were empty, the old wolf was down, and a pup was dragging a leg into impassable slide-rocks.

We reached the old wolf in time to watch a fierce

green fire dying in her eyes. I realized then, and have known ever since, that there was something new to me in those eyes – something known only to her and to the mountain. I was young then, and full of trigger-itch; I thought that because fewer wolves meant more deer, that no wolves would mean hunters' paradise. But after seeing the green fire die, I sensed that neither the wolf nor the mountain agreed with such a view.

Since then I have lived to see state after state extirpate its wolves. I have watched the face of many a newly wolfless mountain, and seen the south-facing slopes wrinkle with a maze of new deer trails. I have seen every edible bush and seedling browsed, first to anaemic desuetude, and then to death. I have seen every edible tree defoliated to the height of a saddle-horn. Such a mountain looks as if someone had given God a new pruning shears, and forbidden Him all other exercise. In the end the starved bones of the hoped-for deer herd, dead of its own too-much, bleach with the bones of the dead sage, or molder under the high-lined junipers.

I now suspect that just as a deer herd lives in mortal fear of its wolves, so does a mountain live in mortal fear of its deer. And perhaps with better cause, for while a buck pulled down by wolves can be replaced in two or three years, a range pulled down by too many deer may fail of replacement in as many decades.

So also with cows. The cowman who cleans his range of wolves does not realize that he is taking over the wolf's job of trimming the herd to fit the range. He has not learned to think like a mountain. Hence we have dustbowls, and rivers washing the future into the sea.

We all strive for safety, prosperity, comfort, long life, and dullness. The deer strives with his supple legs, the cowman with trap and poison, the statesman with pen, the most of us with machines, votes, and dollars, but it all comes to the same thing: peace in our time. A measure of success in this is all well enough, and perhaps is a requisite to objective thinking, but too much safety seems to yield only danger in the long run. Perhaps this is behind Thoreau's dictum: In wildness is the salvation of the world. Perhaps this is the hidden meaning in the howl of the wolf, long known among mountains, but seldom perceived among men.

Escudilla

Life in Arizona was bounded under foot by grama grass, overhead by sky, and on the horizon by Escudilla.

To the north of the mountain you rode on honey-colored plains. Look up anywhere, any time, and you saw Escudilla.

To the east you rode over a confusion of wooded mesas. Each hollow seemed its own small world, soaked in sun, fragrant with juniper, and cozy with the chatter of piñon jays. But top out on a ridge and you at once became a speck in an immensity. On its edge hung Escudilla.

To the south lay the tangled canyons of Blue River, full of whitetails, wild turkeys, and wilder cattle. When you missed a saucy buck waving his goodbye over the skyline, and looked down your sights to wonder why, you looked at a far blue mountain: Escudilla.

To the west billowed the outliers of the Apache National Forest. We cruised timber there, converting the tall pines, forty by forty, into notebook figures representing hypothetical lumber piles. Panting up a canyon, the cruiser felt a curious incongruity between the remoteness of his notebook symbols and the immediacy of sweaty fingers, locust thorns, deer-fly bites, and scolding squirrels. But on the next ridge a cold wind, roaring across a green sea of pines, blew his doubts away. On the far shore hung Escudilla.

The mountain bounded not only our work and our play, but even our attempts to get a good dinner. On winter evenings we often tried to ambush a mallard on the river flats. The wary flocks circled the rosy west, the steel-blue north, and then disappeared into the inky black of Escudilla. If they reappeared on set wings, we had a fat drake for the Dutch oven. If they failed to reappear, it was bacon and beans again.

There was, in fact, only one place from which you did not see Escudilla on the skyline: that was the top of Escudilla itself. Up there you could not see the mountain, but you could feel it. The reason was the big bear.

Old Bigfoot was a robber-baron, and Escudilla was his castle. Each spring, when the warm winds had softened the shadows on the snow, the old grizzly crawled out of his hibernation den in the rock slides and, descending the mountain, bashed in the head of a cow. Eating his fill, he climbed back to his crags, and there summered peaceably on marmots, conies, berries, and roots.

I once saw one of his kills. The cow's skull and neck were pulp, as if she had collided head-on with a fast freight.

No one ever saw the old bear, but in the muddy springs about the base of the cliffs you saw his incredible tracks. Seeing them made the most hard-bitten cowboys aware of bear. Wherever they rode they saw the mountain, and when they saw the mountain they thought of bear. Campfire conversation ran to beef, *bailes*, and bear. Bigfoot claimed for his own only a cow a year, and a few square miles of useless rocks, but his personality pervaded the county.

Those were the days when progress first came to the cow country. Progress had various emissaries:

One was the first transcontinental automobilist. The cowboys understood this breaker of roads; he talked the same breezy bravado as any breaker of broncos.

They did not understand, but they listened to and looked at, the pretty lady in black velvet who came to enlighten them, in a Boston accent, about women's suffrage.

They marveled, too, at the telephone engineer who strung wires on the junipers and brought instantaneous messages from town. An old man asked whether the wire could bring him a side of bacon.

One spring, progress sent still another emissary, a government trapper, a sort of St George in overalls, seeking dragons to slay at government expense. Were there, he asked, any destructive animals in need of slaying? Yes, there was the big bear.

The trapper packed his mule and headed for Escudilla.

In a month he was back, his mule staggering under a heavy hide. There was only one barn in town big enough to dry it on. He had tried traps, poison, and all his usual wiles to no avail. Then he had erected a set-gun in a defile through which only the bear could pass, and waited. The last grizzly walked into the string and shot himself.

It was June. The pelt was foul, patchy, and worthless. It seemed to us rather an insult to deny the last grizzly the chance to leave a good pelt as a memorial to his race. All he left was a skull in the National Museum, and a quarrel among scientists over the Latin name of the skull.

It was only after we pondered on these things that we began to wonder who wrote the rules for progress.

Since the beginning, time had gnawed at the basaltic hulk of Escudilla, wasting, waiting, and building. Time built three things on the old mountain, a venerable aspect, a community of minor animals and plants, and a grizzly.

The government trapper who took the grizzly knew he had made Escudilla safe for cows. He did not know he had toppled the spire off an edifice a-building since the morning stars sang together.

The bureau chief who sent the trapper was a biologist versed in the architecture of evolution, but he did not know that spires might be as important as cows.

He did not foresee that within two decades the cow country would become tourist country, and as such have greater need of bears than of beefsteaks.

The Congressmen who voted money to clear the ranges of bears were the sons of pioneers. They acclaimed the superior virtues of the frontiersman, but they strove with might and main to make an end of the frontier.

We forest officers, who acquiesced in the extinguishment of the bear, knew a local rancher who had plowed up a dagger engraved with the name of one of Coronado's captains. We spoke harshly of the Spaniards who, in their zeal for gold and converts, had needlessly extinguished the native Indians. It did not occur to us that we, too, were the captains of an invasion too sure of its own righteousness.

Escudilla still hangs on the horizon, but when you see it you no longer think of bear. It's only a mountain now.

Chihuahua and Sonora

Guacamaja

The physics of beauty is one department of natural science still in the Dark Ages. Not even the manipulators of bent space have tried to solve its equations. Everybody knows, for example, that the autumn landscape in the north woods is the land, plus a red maple, plus a ruffed grouse. In terms of conventional physics, the grouse represents only a millionth of either the mass or the energy of an acre. Yet subtract the grouse and the whole thing is dead. An enormous amount of some kind of motive power has been lost.

It is easy to say that the loss is all in our mind's eye, but is there any sober ecologist who will agree? He knows full well that there has been an ecological death, the significance of which is inexpressible in terms of contemporary science. A philosopher has called this imponderable essence the *numenon* of material things. It stands in contradistinction to *phenomenon*, which is ponderable and predictable, even to the tossings and turnings of the remotest star.

The grouse is the numenon of the north woods, the blue jay of the hickory groves, the whisky-jack of the muskegs, the piñonero of the juniper foothills. Ornithological texts do not record these facts. I suppose they are new to science, however obvious to the discerning scientist. Be that as it may, I here record the discovery of the numenon of the Sierra Madre: the Thick-billed Parrot.

He is a discovery only because so few have visited his haunts. Once there, only the deaf and blind could fail to perceive his role in the mountain life and landscape. Indeed you have hardly finished breakfast before the chattering flocks leave their roost on the rimrocks and perform a sort of morning drill in the high reaches of the dawn. Like squadrons of cranes they wheel and spiral, loudly debating with each other the question (which also puzzles you) whether this new day which creeps slowly over the canyons is bluer and golder than its predecessors, or less so. The vote being a draw, they repair by separate companies to the high mesas for their breakfast of pine-seed-on-the-half-shell. They have not yet seen you.

But a little later, as you begin the steep ascent out of the canyon, some sharp-eyed parrot, perhaps a mile away, espies this strange creature puffing up the trail where only deer or lion, bear or turkey, is licensed to travel. Breakfast is forgotten. With a whoop and a shout the whole gang is a-wing and coming at you. As they circle overhead you wish fervently for a parrot dictionary. Are they demanding what-the-devil business have you in these parts? Or are they, like an avian chamber-of-commerce, merely making sure you appreciate the glories of their home town, its weather, its citizens, and its glorious future as compared with any and all other times and places whatsoever? It might be either or both. And there flashes through your mind the sad premonition of what will happen when the road is built, and this riotous reception committee first greets the tourist-with-a-gun.

It is soon clear that you are a dull inarticulate fellow, unable to respond by so much as a whistle to the standard amenities of the Sierra morn. And after all, there are more pine cones in the woods than have yet been opened, so let's finish breakfast! This time they may settle upon some tree below the rimrock, giving you the chance to sneak out to the edge and look down. There for the first time you see color: velvet green uniforms with scarlet and yellow epaulets and black helmets, sweeping noisily from pine to pine, but always in formation and always in even numbers. Only once did I see a gang of five, or any other number not comprised of pairs.

I do not know whether the nesting pairs are as noisy as these roistering flocks that greeted me in September. I do know that in September, if there are parrots on the mountain, you will soon know it. As a proper ornithologist, I should doubtless try to describe the call. It superficially resembles that of the piñon jay, but the music of the piñoneros is as soft and nostalgic as the haze hanging in their native canyons, while that of the Guacamaja is louder and full of the salty enthusiasm of high comedy.

In spring, I am told, the pair hunts up a woodpecker hole in some tall dead pine and performs its racial duty in temporary isolation. But what woodpecker excavates a hole large enough? The Guacamaja (as the natives euphoniously call the parrot) is as big as a pigeon, and hardly to be squeezed into a flicker-loft. Does he, with his own powerful beak, perform the necessary enlargement? Or is he dependent on the holes of the imperial woodpecker, which is said to occur in these parts? To some future ornithological visitor I bequeath the pleasant task of discovering the answer.

The Green Lagoons

It is the part of wisdom never to revisit a wilderness, for the more golden the lily, the more certain that someone has gilded it. To return not only spoils a trip, but tarnishes a memory. It is only in the mind that shining adventure remains forever bright. For this reason, I have never gone back to the Delta of the Colorado since my brother and I explored it, by canoe, in 1922.

For all we could tell, the Delta had lain forgotten since Hernando de Alarcon landed there in 1540. When we camped on the estuary which is said to have harbored his ships, we had not for weeks seen a man or a cow, an axe-cut or a fence. Once we crossed an old wagon track, its maker unknown and its errand probably sinister. Once we found a tin can; it was pounced upon as a valuable utensil.

Dawn on the Delta was whistled in by Gambel quail, which roosted in the mesquites overhanging camp. When the sun peeped over the Sierra Madre, it slanted across a hundred miles of lovely desolation, a vast flat bowl of wilderness rimmed by jagged peaks. On the map the Delta was bisected by the river, but in fact the river was nowhere and everywhere, for he could not decide which of a hundred green lagoons offered the most pleasant and least speedy path to the Gulf. So he traveled them all, and so did we. He divided and rejoined, he twisted and turned, he meandered in awesome jungles, he all but ran in circles, he dallied with lovely groves, he got lost and was glad of it, and so were we. For the last word in procrastination, go travel with a river reluctant to lose his freedom in the sea.

'He leadeth me by still waters' was to us only a phrase in a book until we had nosed our canoe through the green lagoons. If David had not written the psalm, we should have felt constrained to write our own. The still waters were of a deep emerald hue, colored by algae, I suppose, but no less green for all that. A verdant wall of mesquite and willow separated the channel from the thorny desert beyond. At each bend we saw egrets standing in the pools ahead, each white statue matched by its white reflection. Fleets of cormorants drove their black prows in quest of skittering mullets; avocets, willets, and yellow-legs dozed one-legged on the bars; mallards, widgeons, and teal sprang skyward in alarm. As the birds took the air, they accumulated in a small cloud ahead, there to settle, or to break back to our rear. When a troop of egrets settled on a far green willow, they looked like a premature snowstorm.

All this wealth of fowl and fish was not for our delectation alone. Often we came upon a bobcat, flattened to some half-immersed driftwood log, paw poised for mullet. Families of raccoons waded the shallows, munching water beetles. Coyotes watched us from inland knolls, waiting to resume their breakfast of mesquite beans, varied, I suppose, by an occasional crippled shore bird, duck, or quail. At every shallow ford were tracks of burro deer. We always examined these deer trails, hoping to find signs of the despot of the Delta, the great jaguar, *el tigre.*

We saw neither hide nor hair of him, but his personality pervaded the wilderness; no living beast forgot his potential presence, for the price of unwariness was death. No deer rounded a bush, or stopped to nibble pods under a mesquite tree, without a premonitory sniff for *el tigre.* No campfire died without talk of him. No dog curled up for the night, save at his master's feet; he needed no telling that the king of cats still ruled the night; that those massive paws could fell an ox, those jaws shear off bones like a guillotine.

By this time the Delta has probably been made safe for cows, and forever dull for adventuring hunters. Freedom from fear has arrived, but a glory has departed from the green lagoons.

When Kipling smelled the supper smokes of Amritsar, he should have elaborated, for no other poet has sung, or smelled, this green earth's firewoods. Most poets must have subsisted on anthracite.

On the Delta one burns only mesquite, the ultimate in fragrant fuels. Brittle with a hundred frosts and floods, baked by a thousand suns, the gnarled imperishable bones of these ancient trees lie ready-to-hand at every camp, ready to slant blue smoke across the twilight, sing a song of teapots, bake a loaf, brown a kettle of quail, and warm the shins of man and beast. When you have ladled a shovelful of mesquite coals under the Dutch oven, take care not to sit down in that spot before bedtime, lest you rise with a yelp that scares the quail roosting overhead. Mesquite coals have seven lives.

We had cooked with white-oak coals in the corn belt, we had smudged our pots with pine in the north woods, we had browned venison ribs over Arizona juniper, but we had not seen perfection until we roasted a young goose with Delta mesquite.

Those geese deserved the best of brownings, for they had bested us for a week. Every morning we watched the cackling phalanx head inland from the Gulf, shortly to return, replete and silent. What rare provender in what green lagoon was the object of their quest? Again and again we moved camp goose-ward, hoping to see them settle, to find their banquet board. One day at about 8 a.m. we saw the phalanx circle, break ranks, sideslip, and fall to earth like maple leaves. Flock after flock followed. At long last we had found their rendezvous.

Next morning at the same hour we lay in wait beside an ordinary-looking slough, its bars covered with yesterday's goosetracks. We were already hungry, for it had been a long tramp from camp. My brother was eating a cold roast quail. The quail was halfway to his mouth when a cackle from the sky froze us to immobility. That quail hung in mid-air while the flock circled at leisure, debated, hesitated, and finally came in. That quail fell in the sand when the guns spoke, and all the geese we could eat lay kicking on the bar.

More came, and settled. The dog lay trembling. We ate quail at leisure, peering through the blind, listening to the small-talk. Those geese were gobbling *gravel*. As one flock filled up and left, another arrived, eager for their delectable stones. Of all the millions of pebbles in the green lagoons, those on this particular bar suited them best. The difference, to a snow goose, was worth forty miles of flying. It was worth a long hike to us.

Most small game on the Delta was too abundant to hunt. At every camp we hung up, in a few minutes' shooting, enough quail for tomorrow's use. Good gastronomy demanded at least one frosty night on the stringer as the necessary interlude between roosting in a mesquite and roasting over mesquite.

All game was of incredible fatness. Every deer laid down so much tallow that the dimple along his backbone would have held a small pail of water, had he allowed us to pour it. He didn't.

The origin of all this opulence was not far to seek.

Every mesquite and every tornillo was loaded with pods. The dried-up mud flats bore an annual grass, the grain-like seeds of which could be scooped up by the cupful. There were great patches of a legume resembling coffeeweed; if you walked through these, your pockets filled up with shelled beans.

I remember one patch of wild melons, or *calabasillas*, covering several acres of mudflat. The deer and coons had opened the frozen fruits, exposing the seeds. Doves and quail fluttered over this banquet like fruit-flies over a ripe banana.

We could not, or at least did not, eat what the quail and deer did, but we shared their evident delight in this milk-and-honey wilderness. Their festival mood became our mood; we all reveled in a common abundance and in each other's well-being. I cannot recall feeling, in settled country, a like sensitivity to the mood of the land.

Camp-keeping in the Delta was not all beer and skittles. The problem was water. The lagoons were saline; the river, where we could find it, was too muddy to drink. At each new camp we dug a new well. Most wells, however, yielded only brine from the Gulf. We learned, the hard way, where to dig for sweet water. When in doubt about a new well, we lowered the dog by his hind legs. If he drank freely, it was the signal for us to beach the canoe, kindle the fire, and pitch the tent. Then we sat at peace with the world while the quail sizzled in the Dutch oven, and the sun sank in glory behind the San Pedro Mártir. Later, dishes washed, we rehearsed the day, and listened to the noises of the night.

Never did we plan the morrow, for we had learned that in the wilderness some new and irresistible distraction is sure to turn up each day before breakfast. Like the river, we were free to wander.

To travel by plan in the Delta is no light matter; we were reminded of this whenever we climbed a cottonwood for a wider view. The view was so wide as to discourage prolonged scrutiny, especially toward the northwest, where a white streak at the foot of the Sierra hung in perpetual mirage. This was the great salt desert, on which, in 1829, Alexander Pattie died of thirst, exhaustion, and mosquitoes. Pattie had a plan: to cross the Delta to California.

Once we had a plan to portage from one green lagoon to a greener one. We knew it was there by the waterfowl hovering over it. The distance was 300 yards through a jungle of *cachinilla*, a tall spear-like shrub which grows in thickets of incredible density. The floods had bent down the spears, which opposed our passage in the manner of a Macedonian phalanx. We discreetly withdrew, persuaded that our lagoon was prettier anyhow.

Getting caught in a maze of *cachinilla* phalanxes

was a real danger that no one had mentioned, whereas the danger we had been warned against failed to materialize. When we launched our canoe above the border, there were dire predictions of sudden death. Far huskier craft, we were told, had been overwhelmed by the tidal bore, a wall of water that rages up the river from the Gulf with certain incoming tides. We talked about the bore, we spun elaborate schemes to circumvent it, we even saw it in our dreams, with dolphins riding its crest and an aerial escort of screaming gulls. When we reached the mouth of the river, we hung our canoe in a tree and waited two days, but the bore let us down. It did not come.

The Delta having no place names, we had to devise our own as we went. One lagoon we called the Rillito, and it is here that we saw pearls in the sky. We were lying flat on our backs, soaking up November sun, staring idly at a soaring buzzard overhead. Far beyond him the sky suddenly exhibited a rotating circle of white spots, alternately visible and invisible. A faint bugle note soon told us they were cranes, inspecting their Delta and finding it good. At the time my ornithology was homemade, and I was pleased to think them whooping cranes because they were so white. Doubtless they were sandhill cranes, but it doesn't matter. What matters is that we were sharing our wilderness with the wildest of living fowl. We and they had found a common home in the remote fast-nesses of space and time; we were both back in the Pleistocene. Had we been able to, we would have bugled back their greeting. Now, from the far reaches of the years, I see them wheeling still.

All this was far away and long ago. I am told the green lagoons now raise cantaloupes. If so, they should not lack flavor.

Man always kills the thing he loves, and so we the pioneers have killed our wilderness. Some say we had to. Be that as it may, I am glad I shall never be young without wild country to be young in. Of what avail are forty freedoms without a blank spot on the map?

Song of the Gavilan

The song of a river ordinarily means the tune that waters play on rock, root, and rapid.

The Rio Gavilan has such a song. It is a pleasant music, bespeaking dancing riffles and fat rainbows laired under mossy roots of sycamore, oak, and pine. It is also useful, for the tinkle of waters so fills the narrow canyon that deer and turkey, coming down out of the hills to drink, hear no footfall of man or horse.

Look sharp as you round the next bend, for it may yield you a shot, and thus save a heart-breaking climb in the high mesas.

This song of the waters is audible to every ear, but there is other music in these hills, by no means audible to all. To hear even a few notes of it you must first live here for a long time, and you must know the speech of hills and rivers. Then on a still night, when the campfire is low and the Pleiades have climbed over rimrocks, sit quietly and listen for a wolf to howl, and think hard of everything you have seen and tried to understand. Then you may hear it – a vast pulsing harmony – its score inscribed on a thousand hills, its notes the lives and deaths of plants and animals, its rhythms spanning the seconds and the centuries.

The life of every river sings its own song, but in most the song is long since marred by the discords of misuse. Overgrazing first mars the plants and then the soil. Rifle, trap, and poison next deplete the larger birds and mammals; then comes a park or forest with roads and tourists. Parks are made to bring the music to the many, but by the time many are attuned to hear it there is little left but noise.

There once were men capable of inhabiting a river without disrupting the harmony of its life. They must have lived in thousands on the Gavilan, for their works are everywhere. Ascend any draw debouching on any canyon and you find yourself climbing little rock terraces or check dams, the crest of one level with the base of the next. Behind each dam is a little plot of soil that was once a field or garden, sub-irrigated by the showers which fell on the steep adjoining slopes. On the crest of the ridge you may find the stone foundations of a watch tower; here the hillside farmer probably stood guard over his polka-dot acrelets. Household water he must have carried from the river. Of domestic animals he evidently had none. What crops did he raise? How long ago? The only fragment of an answer lies in the 300-year-old pines, oaks, or junipers that now find rootage in his little fields. Evidently it was longer ago than the age of the oldest trees.

The deer love to lie on these little terraces. They afford a level bed, free of rocks, upholstered with oak leaves, and curtained by shrubs. One bound over the dam and the deer is out of sight of an intruder.

One day, by aid of a roaring wind, I crept down upon a buck bedded on a dam. He lay in the shade of a great oak whose roots grasped the ancient masonry. His horns and ears were silhouetted against the golden grama beyond, in which grew the green ros-ette of a mescal. The whole scene had the balance of a well-laid centerpiece. I overshot, my arrow splintering on the rocks the old Indian had laid. As the buck bounded down the mountain with a goodbye wave of his snowy flag, I realized that he and I were actors in an allegory. Dust to dust, stone age to stone age, but always the eternal chase! It was appropriate that I missed, for when a great oak grows in what is now my garden, I hope there will be bucks to bed in its fallen leaves, and hunters to stalk, and miss, and wonder who built the garden wall.

Some day my buck will get a .30-.30 in his glossy ribs. A clumsy steer will appropriate his bed under the oak, and will munch the golden grama until it is replaced by weeds. Then a freshet will tear out the old dam, and pile its rocks against a tourist road along the river below. Trucks will churn the dust of the old trail on which I saw wolf tracks yesterday.

To the superficial eye the Gavilan is a hard and stony land, full of cruel slopes and cliffs, its trees too gnarled for post or sawlog, its ranges too steep for pasturage. But the old terrace-builders were not deceived; they knew it by experience to be a land of milk and honey. These twisted oaks and junipers bear each year a crop of mast to be had by wildlings for the pawing. The deer, turkeys, and javelinas spend their days, like steers in a cornfield, converting this mast into succulent meat. These golden grasses conceal, under their waving plumes, a subterranean garden of bulbs and tubers, including wild potatoes. Open the crop of a fat little Mearns' quail and you find an herbarium of subsurface foods scratched from the rocky ground you thought barren. These foods are the motive power which plants pump through that great organ called the fauna.

Every region has a human food symbolic of its fatness. The hills of the Gavilan find their gastronomic epitome in this wise: Kill a mast-fed buck, not earlier than November, not later than January. Hang him in a live-oak tree for seven frosts and seven suns. Then cut out the half-frozen 'straps' from their bed of tallow under the saddle, and slice them transversely into steaks. Rub each steak with salt, pepper, and flour. Throw into a Dutch oven containing deep smoking-hot bear fat and standing on live-oak coals. Fish out the steaks at the first sign of browning. Throw a little flour into the fat, then ice-cold water, then milk. Lay a steak on the summit of a steaming sour-dough biscuit and drown both in gravy.

This structure is symbolic. The buck lies on his mountain, and the golden gravy is the sunshine that floods his days, even unto the end.

Food is the continuum in the Song of the Gavilan. I mean, of course, not only your food, but food for the oak which feeds the buck who feeds the cougar who dies under an oak and goes back into acorns for his erstwhile prey. This is one of many food cycles starting from and returning to oaks, for the oak also feeds the jay who feeds the goshawk who named your river, the bear whose grease made your gravy, the quail who taught you a lesson in botany, and the turkey who daily gives you the slip. And the common end of all is to help the headwater trickles of the Gavilan split one more grain of soil off the broad hulk of the Sierra Madre to make another oak.

There are men charged with the duty of examining the construction of the plants, animals, and soils which are the instruments of the great orchestra. These men are called professors. Each selects one instrument and spends his life taking it apart and describing its strings and sounding boards. This process of dismemberment is called research. The place for dismemberment is called a university.

A professor may pluck the strings of his own instrument, but never that of another, and if he listens for music he must never admit it to his fellows or to his students. For all are restrained by an ironbound taboo which decrees that the construction of instruments is the domain of science, while the detection of harmony is the domain of poets.

Professors serve science and science serves progress. It serves progress so well that many of the more intricate instruments are stepped upon and broken in the rush to spread progress to all backward lands. One by one the parts are thus stricken from the song of songs. If the professor is able to classify each instrument before it is broken, he is well content.

Science contributes moral as well as material blessings to the world. Its great moral contribution is objectivity, or the scientific point of view. This means doubting everything except facts; it means hewing to the facts, let the chips fall where they may. One of the facts hewn to by science is that every river needs more people, and all people need more inventions, and hence more science; the good life depends on the indefinite extension of this chain of logic. That the good life on any river may likewise depend on the perception of its music, and the preservation of some music to perceive, is a form of doubt not yet entertained by science.

Science has not yet arrived on the Gavilan, so the otter plays tag in its pools and riffles and chases the fat rainbows from under its mossy banks, with never a thought for the flood that one day will scour the bank into the Pacific, or for the sportsman who will one day dispute his title to the trout. Like the scientist, he has no doubts about his own design for living. He assumes that for him the Gavilan will sing forever.

Oregon and Utah

Cheat Takes Over

Just as there is honor among thieves, so there is solidarity and co-operation among plant and animal pests. Where one pest is stopped by natural barriers, another arrives to breach the same wall by a new approach. In the end every region and every resource get their quota of uninvited ecological guests.

Thus the English sparrow, rendered innocuous by the shrinkage in horses, was succeeded by the starling, who thrives in the wake of tractors. The chestnut blight, which had no passport beyond the west boundary of chestnuts, is being followed by the Dutch elm disease, with every chance of spreading to the west boundary of elms. The white-pine blister rust, stopped in its westward march by the treeless plains, effected a new landing via the back door, and is now romping down the Rockies from Idaho toward California.

Ecological stowaways began to arrive with the earliest

settlements. The Swedish botanist, Peter Kalm, found most of the European weeds established in New Jersey and New York as early as 1750. They spread as rapidly as the settler's plow could prepare a suitable seedbed.

Others arrived later, from the West, and found thousands of square miles of ready-made seedbed prepared by the trampling hoofs of range livestock. In such cases the spread was often so rapid as to escape recording; one simply woke up one fine spring to find the range dominated by a new weed. A notable instance was the invasion of the intermountain and northwestern foothills by downy chess or cheat grass (*Bromus tectorum*).

Lest you gain too optimistic an impression of this new ingredient of the melting pot, let me say that cheat is not a grass in the sense of forming a live sod. It is an annual weed of the grass family, like foxtail or crabgrass, dying each fall and reseeding that fall or the next spring. In Europe its habitat is the decaying straw of thatched roofs. The Latin word for roof is *tectum*, hence the label 'Brome of the roofs'. A plant that can make a living on the roof of a house can also thrive on this rich but arid roof of the continent.

Today the honey-colored hills that flank the northwestern mountains derive their hue not from the rich and useful bunch-grass and wheatgrass which once covered them, but from the inferior cheat which has replaced these native grasses. The motorist who exclaims about the flowing contours that lead his eye upward to far summits is unaware of this substitution. It does not occur to him that hills, too, cover ruined complexions with ecological face powder.

The cause of the substitution is overgrazing. When the too-great herds and flocks chewed and trampled the hide off the foothills, something had to cover the raw eroding earth. Cheat did.

Cheat grows in dense stands, and each stem bears a mass of prickly awns which render the mature plant inedible to stock. To appreciate the predicament of a cow trying to eat mature cheat, try walking through it in low shoes. All field workers in cheat country wear high boots. Nylons are here relegated to running boards and concrete sidewalks.

These prickly awns cover the autumn hills with a yellow blanket as inflammable as cotton-wool. It is impossible fully to protect cheat country from fire. As a consequence, the remnants of good browse plants, such as sagebrush and bitterbrush, are being burned back to higher altitudes, where they are less useful as winter forage. The lower fringes of pine timber, needed as winter cover for deer and birds, are likewise being singed back to higher levels.

To a summer tourist, the burning of a few bushes

off the foothills may seem a minor loss. He is unaware that, in winter, snow excludes both livestock and game from the higher mountains. Livestock can be fed on valley ranches, but deer and elk must find food in the foothills or starve. The habitable wintering belt is narrow, and the further north one goes, the greater is the disparity between the area of habitable winter range and the area of summer range. Hence these scattering foothill clumps of bitterbrush, sage, and oak, now fast shrinking under the onslaught of cheat fires, are the key to wildlife survival in the whole region. Besides, these scattered bushes often harbor, under their mechanical protection, remnants of native perennial grasses. When the bushes are burned off, these grass remnants succumb to livestock. While the sportsmen and stockmen wrangle over who should move first in easing the burden on the winter range, cheat grass is leaving less and less winter range to wrangle about.

Cheat gives rise to many minor irritations, most of them less important, perhaps, than starving deer or cheat-sores in a cow's mouth, but still worth mentioning. Cheat invades old alfalfa fields and degrades the hay. It blockades newly hatched ducklings from making the vital trek from upland nest to lowland water. It invades the lower fringe of lumber areas, where it chokes out seedling pines and threatens older reproduction with the danger of quick fire.

I experienced a minor irritation myself when I arrived at a 'port of entry' on the northern California border, where my car and baggage were searched by a quarantine officer. He explained politely that California welcomes tourists, but that she must make sure their baggage harbors no plant or animal pests. I asked him what pests. He recited a long list of prospective garden and orchard afflictions, but he did not mention the yellow blanket of cheat, which already extended from his feet to the far hills in every direction.

As is true of the carp, the starling, and the Russian thistle, the cheat-afflicted regions make a virtue of necessity and find the invader useful. Newly sprouted cheat is good forage while it lasts; like as not the lamb chop you ate for lunch was nurtured on cheat during the tender days of spring. Cheat reduces the erosion that would otherwise follow the overgrazing that admitted cheat. (This ecological ring-around-the-rosy merits long thought.)

I listened carefully for clues whether the West has accepted cheat as a necessary evil, to be lived with until kingdom come, or whether it regards cheat as a challenge to rectify its past errors in land-use. I found the hopeless attitude almost universal. There is, as yet, no sense of pride in the husbandry of wild plants and animals, no sense of shame in the proprietorship of a sick landscape. We tilt windmills in behalf of conservation in convention halls and editorial offices, but on the back forty we disclaim even owning a lance.

Manitoba

Clandeboye

Education, I fear, is learning to see one thing by going blind to another.

One thing most of us have gone blind to is the quality of marshes. I am reminded of this when, as a special favor, I take a visitor to Clandeboye, only to find that, to him, it is merely lonelier to look upon, and stickier to navigate, than other boggy places.

This is strange, for any pelican, duckhawk, godwit, or western grebe is aware that Clandeboye is a marsh apart. Why else do they seek it out in preference to other marshes? Why else do they resent my intrusion within its precincts not as mere trespass, but as some kind of cosmic impropriety?

I think the secret is this: Clandeboye is a marsh apart, not only in space, but in time. Only the uncritical consumers of hand-me-down history suppose that 1941 arrived simultaneously in all marshes. The birds know better. Let a squadron of southbound pelicans but feel a lift of prairie breeze over Clandeboye, and they sense at once that here is a landing in the geological past, a refuge from that most relentless of aggressors, the future. With queer antediluvian grunts they set wing, descending in majestic spirals to the welcoming wastes of a bygone age.

Other refugees are already there, each accepting in his own fashion his respite from the march of time. Forster's terns, like troops of happy children, scream over the mudflats as if the first cold melt from the retreating ice sheet were shivering the spines of their minnowy prey. A file of sandhill cranes bugles defiance of whatever it is that cranes distrust and fear. A flotilla of swans rides the bay in quiet dignity, bemoaning the evanescence of swanly things. From the tip of a storm-wracked cottonwood, where the marsh discharges into the big lake, a peregrine stoops playfully at passing fowl. He is gorged with duck meat, but it amuses him to terrorize the squealing teals. This, too, was his after-dinner sport in the days when Lake Agassiz covered the prairies.

It is easy to classify the attitudes of these wildlings, for each wears his heart on his sleeve. But there is one refugee in Clandeboye whose mind I cannot read, for he tolerates no truck with human intruders. Let other birds spill easy confidence to upstarts in overalls, but not the western grebe! Stalk carefully as I will to the bordering reeds, all I get to see is a flash of silver as he sinks, soundless, into the bay. And then, from behind the reedy curtain of the far shore, he tinkles a little bell, warning all his kind of something. Of what?

I've never been able to guess, for there is some barrier between this bird and all mankind. One of my guests dismissed the grebe by checking off his name in the bird list, and jotting down a syllabic paraphrase of the tinkling bell: *'crick-crick'*, or some such inanity. The man failed to sense that here was something more than a bird-call, that here was a *secret* message, calling not for rendition in counterfeit syllables, but for translation and understanding. Alas, I was, and still am, as helpless to translate it or to understand it as he.

As the spring advances, the bell grows persistent; at dawn and at dusk it tinkles from every open water. I infer that the young grebes are now launched in their watery career, and are receiving parental instruction in the grebe philosophy. But to *see* this schoolroom scene, that is not so easy.

One day I buried myself, prone, in the muck of a muskrat house. While my clothes absorbed local color, my eyes absorbed the lore of the marsh. A hen redhead cruised by with her convoy of ducklings, pink-billed fluffs of greenish-golden down. A Virginia rail nearly brushed my nose. The shadow of a pelican sailed over a pool in which a yellow-leg alighted with warbling whistle; it occurred to me that whereas I *write* a poem by dint of mighty cerebration, the yellow-leg *walks* a better one just by lifting his foot.

A mink slithered up the shore behind me, nose in air, trailing. Marsh wrens made trip after trip to a knot in the bulrushes, whence came the clamor of nestlings. I was starting to doze in the sun when there emerged from the open pool a wild red eye, glaring from the head of a bird. Finding all quiet, the silver body emerged: big as a goose, with the lines of a slim torpedo. Before I was aware of when or whence, a second grebe was there, and on her broad back rode two pearly-silver young, neatly enclosed in a corral of humped-up wings. All rounded a bend before I recovered my breath. And now I heard the bell, clear and derisive, behind the curtain of the reeds.

A sense of history should be the most precious gift of science and of the arts, but I suspect that the grebe, who has neither, knows more history than we do. His dim primordial brain knows nothing of who won the Battle of Hastings, but it seems to sense who won the battle of time. If the race of men were as old as the race of grebes, we might better grasp the import of his call. Think what traditions, prides, disdains, and wisdoms even a few self-conscious generations bring to us! What pride of continuity, then, impels this bird, who was a grebe eons before there was a man.

Be that as it may, the call of the grebe is, by some peculiar authority, the sound that dominates and unifies the marshland chorus. Perhaps, by some immemorial authority, he wields the baton for the whole biota. Who beats the measure for the lakeshore rollers as they build reef after reef for marsh after marsh, as age after age the waters recede to lower levels? Who holds sago and bulrush to their task of sucking sun and air, lest in winter the muskrats starve, and the canes engulf the marsh in lifeless jungle? Who counsels patience to brooding ducks by day, and incites bloodthirst in marauding minks by night? Who exhorts precision for the heron's spear, and speed for the falcon's fist? We assume, because all these creatures perform their diverse tasks without admonition audible to us, that they receive none, that their skills are inborn and their industry automatic, that weariness is unknown to the wild. Perhaps weariness is unknown only to grebes; perhaps it is the grebe who reminds them that if all are to survive, each must ceaselessly feed and fight, breed and die.

The marshlands that once sprawled over the prairie from the Illinois to the Athabasca are shrinking northward. Man cannot live by marsh alone, therefore he must needs live marshless. Progress cannot abide that farmland and marshland, wild and tame, exist in mutual toleration and harmony.

So with dredge and dyke, tile and torch, we sucked the cornbelt dry, and now the wheatbelt. Blue lake becomes green bog, green bog becomes caked mud, caked mud becomes a wheatfield.

Some day my marsh, dyked and pumped, will lie forgotten under the wheat, just as today and yesterday will lie forgotten under the years. Before the last mud-minnow makes his last wiggle in the last pool, the terns will scream goodbye to Clandeboye, the swans will circle skyward in snowy dignity, and the cranes will blow their trumpets in farewell.

The Outlook

It is inconceivable to me that an ethical relation to land can exist without love, respect, and admiration for land, and a high regard for its value. By value, I of course mean something far broader than mere economic value; I mean value in the philosophical sense.

Perhaps the most serious obstacle impeding the evolution of a land ethic is the fact that our educational and economic system is headed away from, rather than toward, an intense consciousness of land. Your true modern is separated from the land by many middlemen, and by innumerable physical gadgets. He has no vital relation to it; to him it is the space between cities on which crops grow. Turn him loose for a day on the land, and if the spot does not happen to be a golf links or a 'scenic' area, he is bored stiff. If crops could be raised by hydroponics instead of farming, it would suit him very well. Synthetic substitutes for wood, leather, wool, and other natural land products suit him better than the originals. In short, land is something he has 'outgrown'.

Almost equally serious as an obstacle to a land ethic is the attitude of the farmer for whom the land is still an adversary, or a taskmaster that keeps him in slavery. Theoretically, the mechanization of farming ought to cut the farmer's chains, but whether it really does is debatable.

One of the requisites for an ecological comprehension of land is an understanding of ecology, and this is by no means coextensive with 'education'; in fact, much higher education seems deliberately to avoid ecological concepts. An understanding of ecology does not necessarily originate in courses bearing ecological labels; it is quite as likely to be labeled geography, botany, agronomy, history, or economics. This is as it should be, but whatever the label, ecological training is scarce.

The case for a land ethic would appear hopeless but for the minority which is in obvious revolt against these 'modern' trends.

The 'key-log' which must be moved to release the evolutionary process for an ethic is simply this: quit thinking about decent land-use as solely an economic problem. Examine each question in terms of what is ethically and esthetically right, as well as what is economically expedient. A thing is right when it tends to preserve the integrity, stability, and beauty of the biotic community. It is wrong when it tends otherwise.

It of course goes without saying that economic feasibility limits the tether of what can or cannot be done for land. It always has and it always will. The fallacy the economic determinists have tied around our collective neck, and which we now need to cast off, is the belief that economics determines *all* land-use. This is simply not true. An innumerable host of actions and attitudes, comprising perhaps the bulk of all land relations, is determined by the land-user's tastes and predilections, rather than by his purse. The bulk of all land relations hinges on investments of time, forethought, skill, and faith rather than on investments of cash. As a land-user thinketh, so is he.

I have purposely presented the land ethic as a product of social evolution because nothing so important as an ethic is ever 'written'. Only the most superficial student of history supposes that Moses 'wrote' the Decalogue; it evolved in the minds of a thinking community, and Moses wrote a tentative summary of it for a 'seminar'. I say tentative because evolution never stops.

The evolution of a land ethic is an intellectual as well as emotional process. Conservation is paved with good intentions which prove to be futile, or even dangerous, because they are devoid of critical understanding either of the land, or of economic land-use. I think it is a truism that as the ethical frontier advances from the individual to the community, its intellectual content increases.

The mechanism of operation is the same for any ethic: social approbation for right actions: social disapproval for wrong actions.

By and large, our present problem is one of attitudes and implements. We are remodeling the Alhambra with a steam-shovel, and we are proud of our yardage. We shall hardly relinquish the shovel, which after all has many good points, but we are in need of gentler and more objective criteria for its successful use.